sean scully | recent paintings

sean scully | recent paintings

12 may – 30 june 2006

L | A | LOUVER

FOREWORD

Sean Scully and I both grew up in North London, so our paths could easily have crossed, and perhaps they did. Actually, we met in Los Angeles during the 1970s, and 25 years later, commenced our professional relationship. For me, the wait was well worthwhile. Not only am I now associated with one of the most important abstract painters of our time, but also enjoy the good fortune to be engaged with a complex intellectual mind from whom there is much to learn. Anyone who has been fortunate enough to attend one of Sean Scully's lectures will be able to appreciate this point of view.

In John Yau's catalogue essay, first published in France and revised here on the occasion of this exhibition, we are presented with many associations of ideas which serve to open doors to our greater understanding of Sean Scully's work. I am very grateful to John for his superb text. However, there is no substitute for looking at and spending time with the paintings. Fortunately, with the high degree of international curatorial interest in Sean's work, we have been able to experience his paintings, watercolors and pastel drawings in many museum venues all over the world. Currently, in the United States, a survey of Sean's recent work, entitled "Wall of Light," recently traveled from the Phillips Collection in Washington, D.C., to the Fort Worth Museum of Art, and continues on to the Cincinnati Art Museum this summer, en route to the Metropolitan Museum of Art in New York City. With such an exhibition, a great deal can be learned about the artist's work from the unique nature of each installation.

Simply stated, paintings can take on new identities, or indeed reveal themselves to appear differently from our previous understanding by their presentation within the geography of each new space. In Fort Worth, I came upon a vertical painting entitled, *Barcelona White Bar,* 2004, from the collection of the Sheldon Memorial Art Gallery and Sculpture Garden at the University of Nebraska, which, in its structure, implies the presence of a figure. At the Phillips, this observation escaped my attention. I believe that in this painting lies the key to our current exhibition, both in its physical and formal appearance. In Sean Scully's recent paintings, we can also find that the intersections between the rectangular shapes collide and "bleed" from their grounds within the picture plane.

It may come as a surprise to learn that much of the inspiration for Sean Scully's current work comes from spending time with Caravaggio's paintings in Rome. Caravaggio's use of translucent color serves to sustain our gaze, thereby allowing the dramas depicted to radiate all manner of emotions. These feelings overwhelm their figurative narrative and provide the viewer with an abstract experience, rendering his paintings timeless.

I would like to thank Sean Scully for this beautiful exhibition, and for our association. After all of these years, it is a great privilege to represent him and his work in California.

Peter Goulds Paris, 5 March 2006

RECENT WORKS

Wall of Light Horizon 2005
oil on linen
96 x 144 in. [244 x 366 cm]

Grey Wall Blue 2005
oil on linen
55 $\frac{1}{8}$ x 59 $\frac{1}{4}$ in. [140 x 150.5 cm]

Small Dark Wall 6.05 2005
oil on linen
23 $^7/_8$ x 32 $^1/_4$ in. [60.5 x 82 cm]

Chelsea 11.9.05 2005
pastel on paper
40 x 60 in. [101.6 x 152.4 cm]

Wall of Light Grey Light 9.05 2005
oil on linen
83 $^7/_8$ x 71 $^5/_8$ in. [213 x 182 cm]

Wall of Light Summer 8.05 2005
oil on linen
83 $^7/_8$ x 71 $^5/_8$ in. [213 x 182 cm]

Grey Chelsea Wall of Light
1.12.2005 2005
watercolor on paper
30 x 22 in. [76.2 x 55.9 cm]

GREY CHELSEA WALL OF LIGHT   Sean Scully 1/205

Deep Red 12.15.05 2005
watercolor on paper
30 x 22 in. [76.2 x 55.9 cm]

Wall of Light Roma 2005
oil on linen
83 $^{7}/_{8}$ x 71 $^{5}/_{8}$ in. [213 x 182 cm]

Land Line Grey 9.05 2005
oil on linen
31 $^{7}/_{8}$ x 23 $^{7}/_{8}$ in. [80.5 x 60.5 cm]

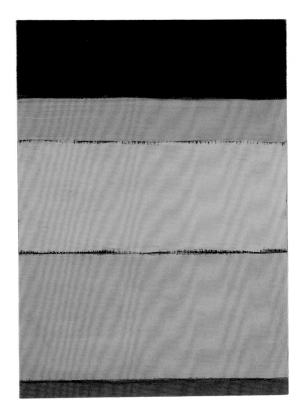

Mirror Orange 2005
oil on linen
45 x 40 in. [114.5 x 101.5 cm]

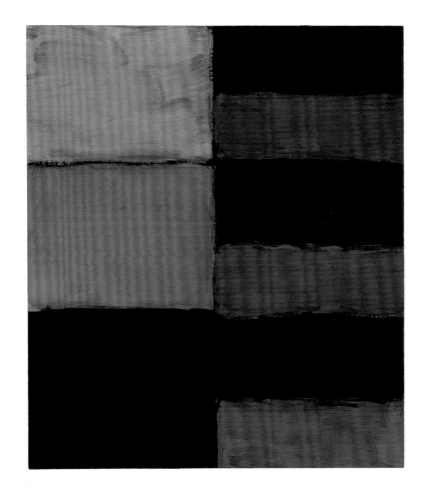

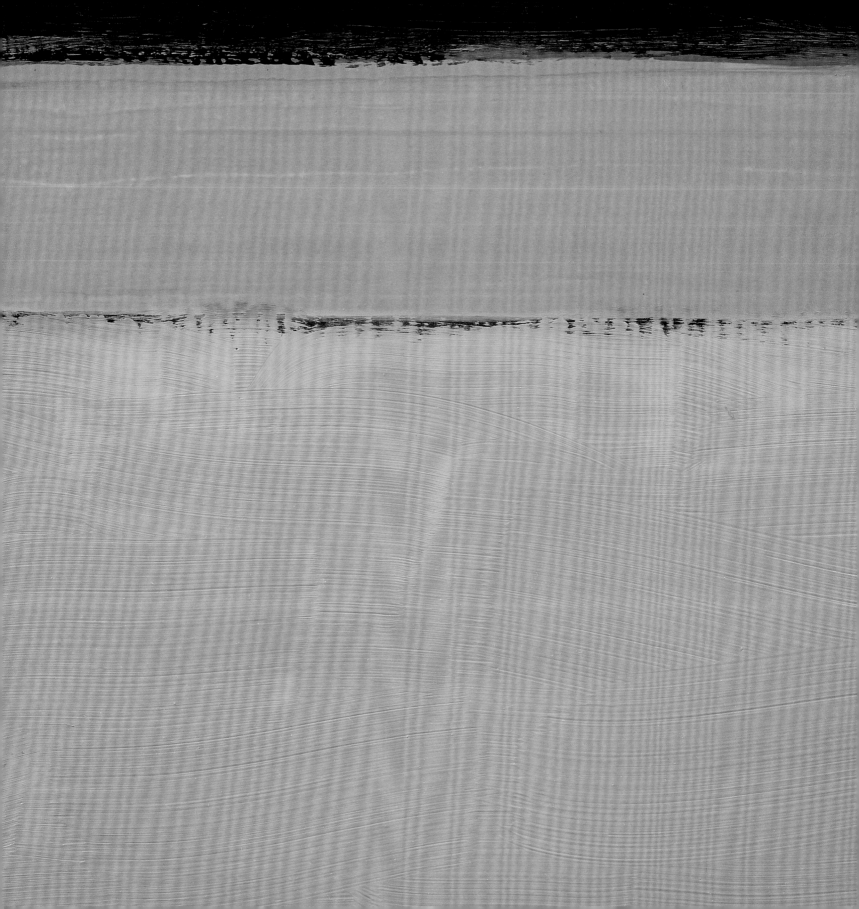

STATES OF DEFIANCE

JOHN YAU

Since 1958, when Jasper Johns first exhibited his encaustic "flags" at the Leo Castelli Gallery, New York, subsequent generations of abstract artists have used the strip (or band) as a compositional element in their paintings. Used as a modular unit, with one placed beside or above another, the stripe can be made to function in different ways. As a simple but immensely malleable form, stripes have been the primary element in a symmetrical pattern; used in a set of interlacing bands; functioned as units in an optical field; been articulated as folds in a curtain; been defined as solid, monochromatic bars of paint, and as semi-transparent bands of light. Just when we think the stripe has been exhausted, having run its course, another artist adapts it to a new idiom, thus both transforming and reinventing it. Sean Scully is such an artist.

Frank Stella, the first artist of his generation to seize upon the formal implications of the stripes in Johns' "flags," emptied out the reference to a real life thing, while maintaining the stripe as structuring element with an abstract design. In his "Black" paintings (1959-1960), Stella used a housepainter's brush to make stripes of equal width, arriving at a symmetrical pattern, the field of which is synonymous with that of the painting. However, immediately after the heraldic "Black" paintings, and the more pictorial stripe paintings he did in 1958, Stella began using masking tape to form crisp, hard-edged stripes, thus removing from his work the last vestiges of expressiveness, and any allusions it might have to Abstract Expressionism. The shift suggests that Stella wanted to achieve a rigorously impersonal, machine-like state in his paintings. It is within this context of the mechanical, and the widespread use of masking tape to arrive at hard-edged, seemingly impersonal stripes

that Sean Scully first emerges as a painter of consequence. His career, however, begins in England, rather than in America. Born in Dublin, Ireland, in 1945, Scully's family moved to London in 1949. After attending various art schools in England, working as a typographic apprentice, and showing his paintings in London, he moved to New York in 1975. Although he was largely unknown in America, he had already mastered an abstract idiom consisting of the use of the stripe, as well as completed an impressive body of work.

Among other things, this body of work signaled Scully's determination to clear a space for himself that was identifiably his own. In contrast to the English Op artist Bridget Riley and the American Color Field artist Kenneth Noland, Scully had introduced an illusionistic space into his stripe paintings. He did so by layering, as well as weaving together, different grid-like patterns consisting of equally spaced stripes. Done in acrylic, the weave of the different sets of colored stripes echoed the weave of the canvas support, as well as articulated a space both materially layered and illusionistic. By using superimposing different grid patterns upon each other, Scully not only evoked urban life, but he also arrived at an illusionistic space without utilizing the devices we associated with illusionism (perspective, for example).

Sean Scully
Bridge 1970
acrylic on canvas
107 $^7/_8$ x 72 in. [274 x 183 cm]

After emigrating to America, Scully understandably changed his work, but not in ways that one might have expected. Instead of aligning himself with artists who were beginning to gain attention for working in a decorative vein, Scully chose to circumscribe his practice, initially working with hard-edged horizontal stripes. At first glance, his paintings from 1975-1980 appear to fit into both the machine-like and Minimalist trajectories that, while still strong, were beginning to lose their dominant position in the art world. Certainly, the shift in Stella's work in the mid 1970s—from the non-illusionistic paintings on canvas to planar wall reliefs, his shift from geometric to decorative motifs, and his use of materials such as glitter—not only contributed to the perception that Minimalism had reached the end of the line, but was also seen as a precedent for the then-emerging Pattern and Decoration movement. Certainly in the wake of Stella's shift, and buttressed by the growing interest in decorative patterning, many understood that change was in the air. Thus, Scully's decision to reduce his options is an anomaly, evidence of the seriousness of his ambition, and a sign of his defiance.

In light of the changes the art world was undergoing when Scully came to America, his paintings from this period (1975-80) are worth reconsidering. In contrast to the abstract wing of Pattern and Decoration, as it was exemplified by Valerie Jaudon, who, in the late seventies in New York, was bending the stripe into a decorative element, Scully was more rigorous and austere in his approach to structuring the paint plane. Jaudon, who worked largely with a monochromatic palette, shifted Stella's stripes away from their formal rigor, bending them into a decorative, overlapping, inter-

lacing pattern. Scully's decision to align two different colored, hard-edged stripes within vertically oriented formats can be seen as evidence of his commitment to high abstraction.

Starting in the late seventies, Scully started to abut two different stripe paintings together. In 1980, he began juxtaposing a set of vertical stripes against a horizontal set. In retrospect, these juxtapositions can be read as Scully's attempt to use a rigorously limited vocabulary to disrupt the cool states associated with Minimalism, as well as challenge the assumptions behind a uniform, all-over field or plane. In terms of their palette, the colors ranged largely from dark greens and browns to grays and blacks. At the same time, to underscore the physicality of the painting, as well as to recover some of the spatiality he had lost when he first began working solely with horizontal stripes, Scully would build up one set of stripes by applying three layers of acrylic, while applying only one layer to make the other. By using only paint to arrive at a differentiated surface, Scully's physically layered paintings can be regarded as a rejoinder to Stella's painted metal reliefs.

Scully's willful juxtaposition of two self-sufficient sets of stripes not only distinguished him from those artists involved with Pattern and Decoration, but also from those artists who limited themselves to monochrome as a way of further extending Minimalism into a theoretical domain. By juxtaposing two physically different stripes together, as well as by juxtaposing two canvases together, Scully extended the possibility of the modular unit into a more physical, more expansive territory, a place of speculation that would eventually make his own. For one thing, by juxtaposing and abutting canvases, Scully equated paintings with building construction and architecture, as well as with rupture and incommensurability.

II Scully's career shifts between the poles of reduction and expansion. After immigrating to America, he severely reduced his options and worked within a narrow range of colors before he allowed himself to expand upon them. Consequently, after working solely with horizontal stripes, and a palette of mostly nocturnal and earth colors, he redefined his possibilities by juxtaposing horizontal stripes against vertical ones. In doing so, he not only transformed the modular unit, the stripe, into distinct sets, but he also established a way of expanding outward, of no longer being confined to a single support. *Backs and Fronts* (1981), for example, consists of ten different panels and widths. The artist has connected the use of a modular unit to construction, but not to reproducibility and the machine-like. One could say Scully is evoking unregulated construction, and that which is built with whatever is at hand.

The current of expansion, of feeling that there are no limits but the actual ones imposed by the world, and the specific site, impart a feeling of willfulness to the work, at once brute and brooding. The viewer feels as if Scully's work arises out of an attempt to break free of the assumptions of Minimalism, as well as more personal ones. In addition, Scully's use of stripes suggests that he knows the attempt is futile, and refuses to succumb to despair. Originality was never the issue, only the possibility

that the painting could become a palpable thing in this world, something that embodied states of feeling and perceiving, the physical and the visual.

The other more significant change that Scully effected in his work occurred in 1980, when he switched from acrylic to oil. This decision enabled him to slowly reintroduce into his work much of what he had lost or deliberately suppressed when he gave up illusionism. Thus, color, drawing, proportion, layering and varying degrees of light enter into the work. In doing so, he gained the possibility of expressiveness. In recovering these possibilities, as well as recontextualizing them within a more expressive approach, Scully sets himself apart from those artists who tried to either offset or remove evidence of the hand in abstract painting. In contrast to his American peers, he didn't feel the need to tacitly reify Clement Greenberg's formalist dogma regarding flatness and the obsolescence of the hand. Scully's reintroduction of the hand, of matter-of-fact, yet energetic, brushy surfaces, is important for a number of reasons, one of which is an implicit criticism of the trajectory of abstraction as exemplified by Peter Halley and Joseph Marioni. As Scully understood, abstraction's goal was neither a utopian (or dystopian) domain nor an impersonal one.

Beyond Scully's implicit critique looms a larger issue, which is that history doesn't progress in a linear fashion, particularly as defined by both formalist critics and theoreticians of the postmodern. Rather, his paintings convey the likelihood that he believes history is circular. In this regard he shares something with his fellow Irishman, James Joyce, whose interest in the eighteenth century philosopher Giambattista Vico and his theories regarding the cyclical nature of history influenced the writing of *Finnegans Wake.* The other parallel they share is that both collapse the figure-ground relationship, so that they become interchangeable. On a formal level, this circularity is in keeping with Vico's view that history is the unfolding of overlapping, interlocking, cyclical patterns. On a personal level, Scully's collapsing of the figure-ground relationship conveys his awareness of mortality; one literally becomes part of the ground.

III Even if one doesn't subscribe to either the formalist or postmodern models of history, it is possible to misunderstand the nature of Scully's achievement. Certainly, his own early rejection of Greenbergian formalism, and his reintroduction of a layered, illusionistic space into his weave paintings should have made it evident that he wasn't trying to fit. Taking this aspect of Scully's early work into account, it becomes apparent that my harsh criticism of his work of the 1980s was misplaced. In fact, in his recent work, it is increasingly evident that in setting out to recover aspects of abstract painting that had been jettisoned, suppressed, or marginalized by the generations to emerge in the wake of Abstract Expressionism, Scully wasn't, as I first believed, being nostalgic. In his work, he didn't look back. Rather, by working with a narrow, yet surprisingly malleable vocabulary, he was, and is, deeply committed to re-envisioning history, which is to say he wants to make viable again what many have presumed was lost. This, I think, is one of the central features of his achievement. The question that has to be answered is, how has Scully re-envisioned

history? And, in his re-envisioning, what has he added to the sum of our knowledge that is unmistakably his? Here, I would suggest that around 1980, Scully took up where Stella left off, near the outset of his career. However, in order to not reprise Stella's early, pre-black paintings, such as *Coney Island* (1958), with its monochromatic rectangle floating in a field of horizontal stripes, *Astoria* (1958), with the brushy, dripping facture of its horizontal stripes, and *Delta* (1958), with its asymmetrical design, Scully had to bring new to bear in his work. Moreover, it couldn't simply be new; whatever he introduced also had to be convincing in its necessity.

Sean Scully
Inset #2 1973
acrylic on canvas
96 x 96 in. [243.8 x 243.8 cm]

As early as 1973, while still living in England, Scully made a painting, *Inset 2,* in which he juxtaposed a pattern of verticals and horizontals, within and against a pattern made largely of made diagonals. While smaller, scumbled pattern of right angles seems to float in front of the hard-edged diagonal pattern, the viewer detects echoes of the larger pattern within the interstices of the larger, diagonal pattern. These echoes underscore Scully's interest in paintings being a record of decisions made, a palimpsest. At the same time, not only was the handling different in the smaller rectangle, but it also anticipates the changes that began transpiring in Scully's work around 1980. Not only does the "inset" disrupt the all-overness of the painting, as well as the privileging of one over the other, but it also anticipates such painters as Fabian Marcaccio, who tries to subvert a painting's authority by exposing both its interior skeleton and skin. The difference is that Scully's disruptions occur within a Minimalist syntax, suggesting that this too hasn't been played out.

In Scully's most arresting paintings, the patterns or repeating motifs are disturbed by another pattern or motif that has been set against it or within its field. His best work embodies such characteristics as incongruity, dissonance, an imperfect mirroring, and a resistance to stability that one associates with the repetition of modular units within an all-over, non-hierarchical composition. Such disturbances stir the viewer from the contemplative states associated with reductive painting, and the work of Agnes Martin, say, to something more active, more open-ended. The paintings induce the viewer to consider both their self-sufficient existence and their allusions to a world marked by one's inchoate feelings. Typically, he tries to reconcile feelings of disorientation and imbalance with those stirred up by the rhythmic placement of different-sized bands of paint and compressed sense of space. However, because Scully's structures neither cohere into a single, all-over image, nor disintegrate into completely separate parts, the viewer never reconciles feelings of imbalance and balance. Rather, the viewer is confronted by the painting's constant friction, which borders on a respectful but irresolvable antagonism.

One cannot help but recognize Scully's determined willfulness in juxtaposing different sets of similarly sized bands together. Often, the juxtapositions underscore a misalignment between the two sets of stripes. The world these paintings embody never quite melds together, never quite

coheres. In the works of the early 1980s, it is apparent that Scully is being highly critical of both Stella's early commitment to containing bright disturbances within non-expressive designs, and to his subsequent incorporation of sculptural motifs that mimicked the painterly brushstroke. In contrast to the nearly cheerless charm of Stella's palette, Scully's choice of colors was more moody, more emotional, and more suggestive.

For Scully, formalism, and its rejection of spatiality, drawing and the subjective, was something to go against, not in a reactionary way, but in a way that was secure in both its critique and its creativity. The subjective in favor of the objective, was something to go against, not in a reactionary way, but in a way that was secure in both its critique and its creativity. For his paintings to be successful, they had to be complete in their criticism of Stella's paintings, but they had to embody a viable alternative, a total worldview. Thus, Scully, who was determined to become independent of formalism, revealed himself to be interested in gaining access to subjective states, something which couldn't be repeated from painting to painting and which we associate with Abstract Expressionism. Thus, he couldn't simply fill a shaped canvas with different colors, as Stella had done in the Protractor series (1967-71). He had to be more specific and more open, as well as less methodical than that.

In Scully's paintings, there is a brooding assertiveness, as well as an inherent awkwardness, that conveys a state of defiance tinged with vulnerability. In his use of insets, defiance and intervention not only become inherent aspects of the painting, but they also remind us that no surface is inviolable. Among other things, the paintings evoke the patchwork responses we have to our crumbling urban environment, the intervention it is necessary for us to make in order to prevent further decay.

In both their blunt physicality and their distinct juxtapositions of colors and tonalities, Scully's paintings most often convey somberness. Black is a recurring color. However, Scully's paintings are not about the death of painting. Their elegiac nature strikes us as being more about the difficulties of living than about the difficulties of art. Scully has synthesized such as his collapsing of the figure-ground, and his moody colors, to subjective states and ultimate inability of painting to overcome mortality.

IV   In recent years, Scully's need to disrupt, to misalign, and subvert any evidence of an all-over pattern has led him to establish a disordered geometry in a palette that is both gloomy and fiery. In his Mirrors, he deploys multiple panels that echo but do not mirror each other. In the tension he establishes between the desire for self-contained order and the realization that the randomness of life infiltrates everything, including art, the viewer recognizes that what the painting mirrors is not itself, but the world in which it exists, and of which it is a part. In another ongoing series collectively titled "Wall of Light," he rotates different sets of bands (either a pair or a set of three) across the entire plane. Other colors glow and seethe in the crevices between these sets, which are abutted together as firmly as Babylonian stones. In using a palette that ranges from black to sunset red, and includes colors such as umber, orange, tan, gray and gray blue, Scully conveys a state of change

and volatility. One senses that these colors have to do with the space where the destabilized exterior world meets his solemn interior one.

There seems to be no overall design into which the bands can be made to settle, only a state of continuous change, shifts and disruption. The rotating puzzle-like effect is mesmerizing. Our eyes keep moving, as we both take apart and reassemble the planar structure in our mind's eye. Engaged by Scully's attentiveness to tonality, contrast and structure, we become acutely attuned to every aspect of the painting, to the broad brushwork, to the surfaces that range from viscous to scumbled, and to the layers of colors, and the coloristic shifts that occur between one set of bands and another. The paintings have built into their structure recognition of time and time passing. Scully's paintings compel the viewer to begin dissecting them, to taking them apart and examining their constituent elements. We don't look at his walls of light, we look at ourselves looking at them, and recognize that we can't see beyond them; we can see only this portion of something far more vast and limitless than either our eyes or mind can comfortably comprehend.

There is no vantage point from which an entire painting, even one as intimate in scale as *Small Dark Wall* (2005) can be seen. The layering of colors and subtly changing physicality of the surface, as well as the shifting tonalities and sense of dissonance that has been arrived at, all contribute to our feelings of disquiet. Our attention moves from the bands to the edges, from the ruptured surface to the colors flaring along the seams. At the same time, there is a sense of acceptance in these paintings, recognition

that harmony cannot be imposed upon the unruly world. For by making
his paintings synonymous with awkwardness, defiance, disruption, and
precariousness, Scully reveals the inherent torment of being human.

In a large painting such as *Wall of Light Horizon* (2005), fiery reds bleed
through the seams between the black, dark gray and umber bands.
An intense heat lies on the other side of this wall, this construction made
of planes of paint. Once we thought that the walls we built would outlast
us all, but now we know that was never true. Architecture is one of our
most fragile endeavors. The bands seem both solid and susceptible.
This is the conundrum we must keep learning over and over, that what we
build will eventually be ruined. It is a fact that Scully has neither avoided
nor denied. He is a painter who keeps looking and looking, and does not
turn his eyes away.

John Yau *is a poet and critic whose latest book of poems is* Ing Grish, *with art-
work by Thomas Nozkowski, published by Saturnalia Books in 2005. He teaches
at Mason Gross School of the Arts at Rutgers University, and lives in Manhattan.*

*Note: An earlier version of "States of Defiance" was published by Galerie Lelong
in 1999. The essay has been rewritten for the purposes of this exhibition.*

SELECTED WORKS
FROM L.A. LOUVER

Green Pale Light 2002
oil on linen
84 x 96 in. [213.4 x 243.8 cm]
Private collection, Los Angeles, CA

Big Grey Robe 2002
oil on linen
90 x 72 in. [228.6 x 182.9 cm]
Collection of the Museum of Modern Art, New York
Fractional and promised gift of Edward R. Broida

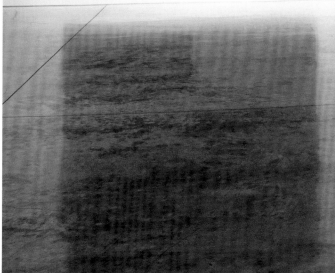

Four Dark Mirrors 2002
oil on linen (four panels)
each: 108 x 96 in. [274.3 x 243.8 cm]
Collection of the Museum of Fine Arts, Houston
Museum purchase with funds provided by the
Caroline Wiess Law Accessions Endowment Fund, 2005.364

Art Horizon II 2002
suite of 12 cibachrome prints
mounted on aluminum
edition of 5 + 2 artist proofs
each: 23 ½ x 12 in. [60 x 30 cm]

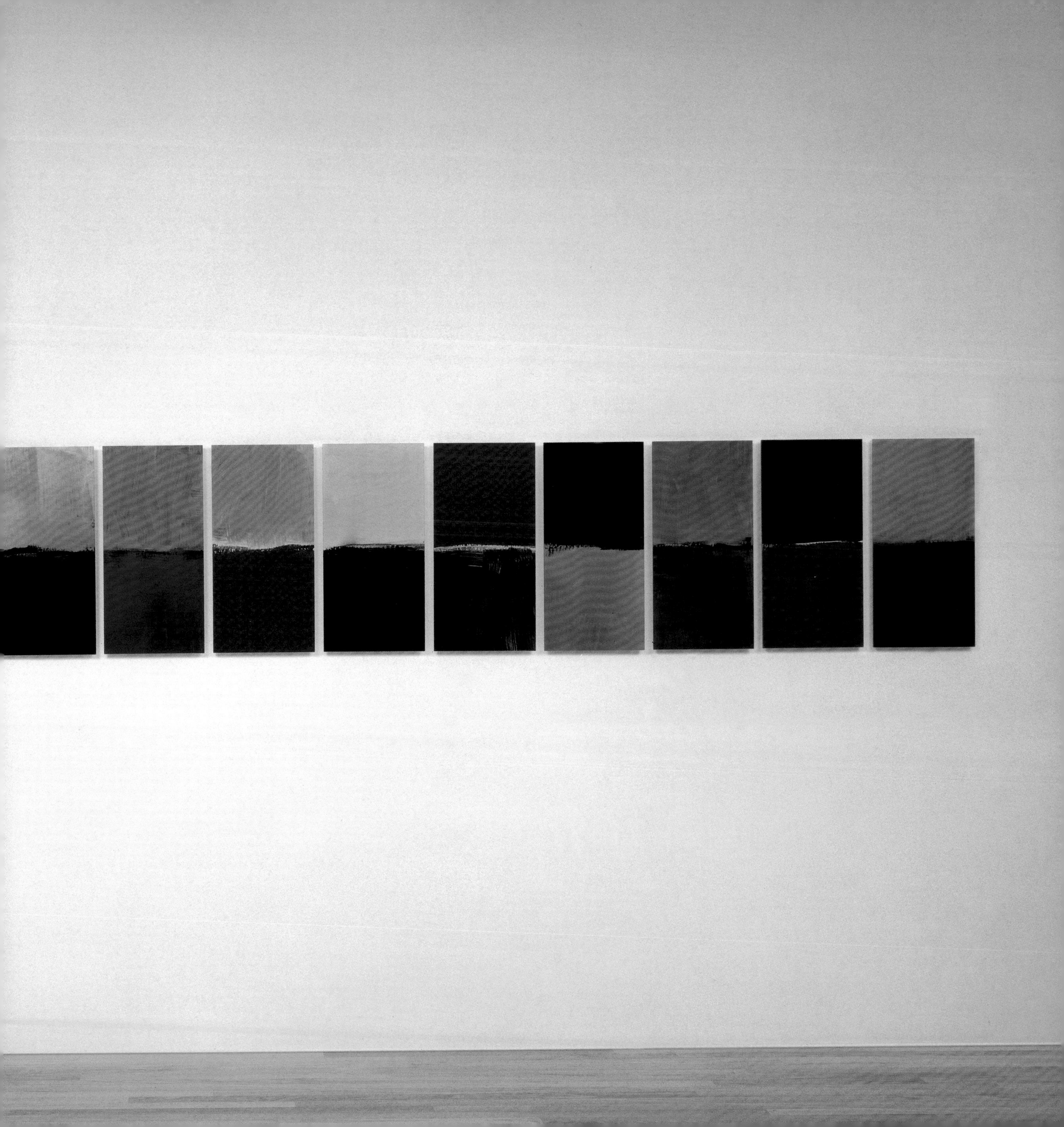

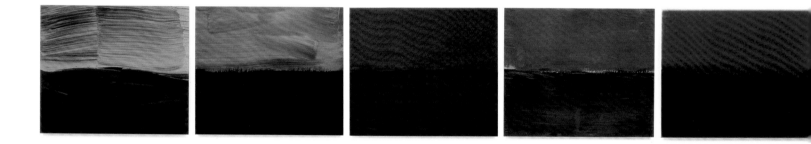

Art Horizon III 2002
suite of 10 cibachrome prints
mounted on aluminum
edition of 5 + 2 artist proofs
each: 19 ½ x 23 ½ in. [50 x 60 cm]

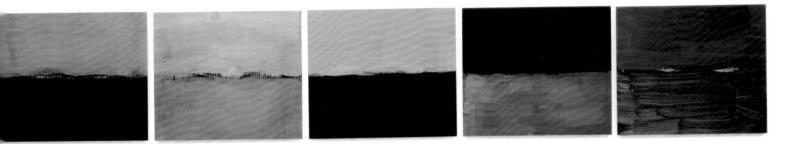

Towers I 2003
suite of 9 cibachrome prints on aluminum
edition of 10 + 2 artist proofs
each: 35 $\frac{1}{2}$ x 13 $\frac{7}{8}$ in. [90.2 x 35.2 cm]

Wall of Light, Desert Day 2003
oil on linen
108 x 132 in. [274.3 x 335.3 cm]
Collection of the National Gallery of Australia, Canberra
Purchased for the National Gallery of Australia
in honour of Dr. Brian Kennedy, Director 1997-2004,
with contributions from Members
of the NGA Council and Foundation 2004

SEAN SCULLY
PUBLIC COLLECTIONS

UNITED STATES AND SOUTH AMERICA

Albright-Knox Art Gallery Buffalo, New York

Art Institute of Chicago Chicago, Illinois

Art Gallery of Ontario Ontario, Canada

Carnegie Museum of Art Pittsburgh, Pennsylvania

Cantor Center for Visual Arts, Stanford University Stanford, California

Centro Cultural de Arte Contemporaneo Mexico City, Mexico

Chase Manhattan Bank New York, New York

Chemical Bank New York, New York

Cincinnati Art Museum Cincinnati, Ohio

Cleveland Museum of Art Cleveland, Ohio

Contemporary Museum Honolulu, Hawaii

Corcoran Gallery of Art Washington, D.C.

Dallas Museum of Art Dallas, Texas

Denver Art Museum Denver, Colorado

Des Moines Art Center De Moines, Iowa

First Bank Minneapolis Minneapolis, Minnesota

Fogg Art Museum, Harvard University Cambridge, Massachusetts

Ft. Lauderdale Museum of Art Ft. Lauderdale, Florida

Guggenheim Museum New York, New York

Hirshhorn Museum and Sculpture Garden Washington, D.C.

High Museum of Art Atlanta, Georgia

Modern Art Museum of Fort Worth Fort Worth, Texas

Mellon Bank Pittsburgh, Pennsylvania

Metropolitan Museum of Art New York, New York

Miami Art Museum Miami, Florida

Museo de Arte Contemporaneo Caracas, Venezuela

Museo de Arte Contemporaneo Monterrey, Mexico

Museo de Arte Moderno Col. Bosques de Chapultepec, Mexico

Museum of Fine Art, Boston Boston, Massachusetts

Museum of Fine Arts, Houston Houston, Texas

Museum of Modern Art New York, New York

National Gallery of Art Washington, D.C.

Orlando Museum of Art Orlando, Florida

Paine Webber Group, Inc. New York, New York

Philip Morris, Inc. New York, New York

The Phillips Collection Washington, D.C.

Santa Barbara Museum of Art Santa Barbara, California

Sheldon Memorial Art Gallery and Sculpture Garden, University of Nebraska, Lincoln, Nebraska

Smithsonian American Art Museum Washington, D.C.

Snite Museum of Art Notre Dame, Indiana

San Diego Museum of Art San Diego, California

The Saint Louis Art Museum Saint Louis, Missouri

Walker Art Center Minneapolis, Minnesota

Yale University Art Gallery New Haven, Connecticut

EUROPE

Abbot Hall Art Gallery Kendal, England

Grafische Sammlung Albertina Vienna, Austria

Arts Council of Great Britain London, England

Banque Européenne d'Investissement Luxembourg

Bayrische Staatsgemaeldesammlung Munich, Germany

Bibliothèque Nationale de France Paris, France

Birmingham Museum of Art Birmingham, England

The British Council London, England

Ceolfrith Art Center Sunderland, England

Chilliada-Leku Hernani, Spain

Consejería de Cultura Santander, Spain

Contemporary Arts Society London, England

Council of National Academic Awards London, England

Crawford Municipal Art Gallery Cork, Ireland

The DG Bank Collection Frankfurt, Germany

Eastern Arts Association Cambridge, England

Ecole d'Arts Plastiques Châtelierault, France

Fitzwilliam Museum Cambridge, England

La Fondation Edelman Lausanne, Switzerland

Foundation Stiftelsen Focus Boras, Sweden

Fundacio La Caixa Barcelona, Spain

Fundación Caixa Galicia La Coruña, Spain

Galleria D'Arte Moderna Bologna, Italy

Gallery of Modern Art László Vass Collection Veszprém, Hungary

Hôtel des Arts Toulon, France

Hunterian Art Gallery Glasgow, Scotland

Hugh Lane Municipal Gallery Dublin, Ireland

Institute Valencià d' Arte Modern Valencià, Spain

Irish Museum of Modern Art Dublin, Ireland

Kunsthalle Bielefeld Bielefeld, Germany

Kunstsammlung Nordrhein-Westfalen Düsseldorf, Germany

Kunsthaus Zürich Zürich, Switzerland

Kunst und Museumsverein Wuppertal Wuppertal, Germany

Laing Art Gallery Newcastle-Upon-Tyne, England

Leicesterchire Educational Authority Leicester, England

Louisiana Museum Humlebaek, Denmark

Manchester City Art Gallery Manchester, England

Museum Folkwang Essen, Germany

Musee du Val de Marne Ivry-sur-Seine, France

Musee du Dessin et de l'Estampe Originale Gravelines, France

Musee Jenisch Vevey, Switzerland

Museo Nacional Centro de Arte Reina Sofia Madrid, Spain

Museu d'Art Contemporàni de Barcelona Barcelona, Spain

Museum Moderner Kunst, Stiftung Ludwig Vienna, Austria

Museum Pfalzgalerie Kaiserslautern, Germany

National Museum Cardiff Cardiff, Wales

Neue Galerie der Stadt Linz Linz, Austria

Northern Arts Association Newcastle-Upon-Tyne, England

Ruhr Universitat Bochum, Germany

Saastamoisen Saatio Helsinki, Finland

Sala Rekalde Bilbao, Spain

Sammlung Essl Vienna, Austria

Sara Hilden Art Museum Tampere, Finland

Staatsgalerie Stuttgart, Germany

Staatliche Museen Kassel, Neue Galerie Kassel, Germany

Städtische Galerie im Lenbachhaus Munich, Germany

Tate Gallery London, England

Ulster Museum Belfast, Ireland

Victoria and Albert Museum London, England

Whitworth Art Gallery Manchester, England

Zentrum für Kunst und Medien Technologie Karlsruhe, Germany

University of Limmerick Limmerick, Ireland

AUSTRALIA

National Gallery of Australia Canberra

National Gallery of Victoria Felton Bequest, Melbourne

Power Institute of Contemporary Art Sydney

JAPAN

Nagoya City Art Museum Nagoya

Tokyo International Forum Tokyo

SEAN SCULLY
EXHIBITION CHECK LIST

Wall of Light Horizon
2005, oil on linen
96 x 144 in. [244 x 366 cm]

Grey Wall Blue
2005, oil on linen
55 1/8 x 59 1/4 in. [140 x 150.5 cm]

Small Dark Wall 6.05
2005, oil on linen
23 7/8 x 32 1/4 in. [60.5 x 82 cm]

Chelsea 11.9.05
2005, pastel on paper
40 x 60 in. [101.6 x 152.4 cm]

Wall of Light Grey Light 9.05
2005, oil on linen
83 7/8 x 71 5/8 in. [213 x 182 cm]

Wall of Light Summer 8.05
2005, oil on linen
83 7/8 x 71 5/8 in. [213 x 182 cm]

Grey Chelsea Wall of Light 1.12.2005
2005, watercolor on paper
30 x 22 in. [76.2 x 55.9 cm]

Deep Red 12.15.05
2005, watercolor on paper
30 x 22 in. [76.2 x 55.9 cm]

Wall of Light Roma
2005, oil on linen
83 7/8 x 71 5/8 in. [213 x 182 cm]

Land Line Grey 9.05
2005, oil on linen
31 7/8 x 23 7/8 in. [80.5 x 60.5 cm]

Mirror Orange
2005, oil on linen
45 x 40 in. [114.5 x 101.5 cm]

CREDITS

SEAN SCULLY
RECENT PAINTINGS

Library of Congress Control Number:
2005904769
ISBN 0-9765585-5-6

Design by Stefan G. Bucher
for 344design.com
Printing by Typecraft, Wood & Jones
Pasadena, California

L.A. Louver
45 North Venice Boulevard
Venice, CA 90291
Tel 310.822.4955
Fax 310.821.7529
www.lalouver.com

DETAILS

THANK YOU

Nicole Hayes
Frank Hutter
Liliane Tomasko
Lisa Jann
Chris Pate
Dana Gildenhorn

SEAN SCULLY
ARAN ISLANDS, JUNE 2005
PHOTOGRAPH BY LILIANE TOMASKO

L | A | LOUVER

30TH ANNIVERSARY
LALOUVER.COM